T0137522

DEFENSE AGAINST

THE

"SPIRIT BREAKERS"

(A POETIC GUIDE TO HUMANITY)

BY

CRYSTAL STEWART

iUniverse, Inc.
New York   Bloomington

Defense Against The "Spirit Breaker's"
A Poetic Guide To Humanity

iUniverse books may be ordered through booksellers or by contacting:

iUniverse
1663 Liberty Drive
Bloomington, IN 47403
www.iuniverse.com
1-800-Authors (1-800-288-4677)

ISBN: 978-1-4401-1868-5 (pbk)
ISBN: 978-1-4401-1869-2 (ebk)

Printed in the United States of America

iUniverse rev. date: 3/17/2009

DEFENSE AGAINST

THE

"SPIRIT BREAKERS"

(A POETIC GUIDE TO HUMANITY)

BY

CRYSTAL STEWART

This is for all the Spirit Builders in my life, especially you MJ, Thank you for directing my light through your light.

"Ad maiorem Dei gloriam."

Preface

This world in its circler manner, with its vast countries, and cities going on forever, distance our many spirits, even several miles, but regardless, we as spirits, are connected beyond Divinity's beautiful Universe. Each of us hidden behind our mortal attire, beneath our varied colors of skin, as each of our mortal's energy, pulses through us, pumping deep blue blood, until a crashing conflict breaks the surface against the rapture, we all bleed many colors red, no other. Life's vital organs function the same, well at least for the most part, (nobody is perfect), we as mortals, need the same elements to survive, within this "Mortal Spectrum", but go deeper, to the core of our souls, through the depths of our minds. Let go, open your mind, better yet strengthen your mind, and open your heart.

Now consider this; if our mortal bodies were stripped away, and our carcass's suddenly disintegrated and blew into the wind today; what remains? Our spirits! Regardless of our own gender, social stature, self-beliefs, or the pressures of distasteful individuals or organized assemblages, we are all equal. Regardless of where you believe your "light" or spirit derives from, we are all connected equally, and are created equally through a heavenly power. Our spirits posses this incredible power.

My spirits maker instilled within my spirit, before this time, and now, the knowledge of what is right from wrong. This mortal world has tainted my true spirit, with this; time is my chance to change.

As Gandhi quoted: "Almost anything you do seems insignificant, it is very important that you do it, you must be the change you wish to see in the world".

Contents

Chapter 1
"Childs Innocence"

We are born innocent
Little hands
Clapping
With each other
Then our fists are thrust against
Each other
Attitudes of losers
Thinking that we are winning the game
When we just inflict pain
Upon another's heart
Tearing the world apart
When we accepted each other from the start
Now we are pushing each other
Over the edge
Confiscating grudges
Without dread, of what a second may bring
Not stopping for a moment to think
Of the friend, we held so dear
The selfishness is clear
Clouded images
Tainted views
How could something so beautiful
Become so twisted
A child's innocence
Once gifted
Now taking so much for granted
Born innocence so slanted

"Children are a heritage of the Lord". (Psalm 127:3)

What is the Depth of a person's true self? Before the first breath taken, as motif's backdrop changes from blue to red? Is it the stages of the becoming whole? Growing from an infant to unknown years? Are these years undetermined? Or is the pathway already drawn upon a tapestry? Only visible to the Angels, or Christ himself? Are we Spirits? Shifting with learning? Amongst the battle of Good versus Evil?

As children, we are blinded from the reality of the world, falling into traits, and beliefs.

Simply just walking through life, learning from examples. It is very crucial that we raise our children in a dignified manner. It is so very important in the manner of which we teach our children. Children are born innocent; their spirits are not yet tainted with the ugliness of this mortal world. Immorality has not yet left its impure footprint upon their minds, and in their hearts. A child's spirit reflects Christ's own likeliness; to look upon a child's face is to be looking upon Christ's face. A child's spirit symbolizes purity, innocence and unconditional love. As parents, we should be setting examples for our children, as well as other parents, and their children.

"Verily I say unto you, whosoever shall not receive the kingdom of God as a little child, he shall not enter therein". (St. Mark 10:15)

"The spirit itself beareth witness with our spirit, that we are the children of God". (Romans 8:16)

"Be ye therefore followers of God, as dear children". (Ephesians 5:1)

"How excellent is thy loving kindness, O God! Therefore the children of men put their trust under the shadows of thy wings". (Psalm 36:7)

Chapter 2
"Alter thy Disappointments"

With once ye walked
Where angels sang
But now to hang thy head
With blame
For where did once
All souls have come
Have thou forgotten
Amongst your shame
The darkened path
Has seemed
Much shorter
But with this
If you teach
Follow
The weight you bare
The heaviness upon your shoulders
An affliction
Lost
If ye find yourself

Through humility
Doctrine
Which has always been
Except
Yearn
To be renewed
Just as the child
Still remains true

Within thy self
Share with the world

Experience is an example that can be a great diversion for others who follow such as your children, family, and friends. I say diversion, but I really mean more less a detour towards a greater life experience, or possibly a shorter route to true

happiness. Give of yourself to others. Enlighten another's journey through life from your mistakes, disappointments, pain, and most importantly your happiness. Whether you have children or not, teach another's inner child, and bare witness to the truth of innocence, we all have once forgotten. Learn from your mistakes, do not take previous trials for granted. God has given us each moment to redeem ourselves as well as giving us the opportunity in serving with the redemption of others.

"Whosoever therefore shall humble himself as this little child, the same is greatest in the kingdom of heaven". (Matthew 18:4)

"And if children, then heirs; heirs of God, and joint-heirs with Christ; if so be that we suffer with him, that we may be also glorified together". (Romans 8:17)

Chapter 3
"The Discriminator"

Facts of fury flood my mind
I fall
I search
But still can't find
The words or dialect
That is "socially" proper
Even with sincerity
The accusations still plunder
Nuisance, with innocent attempts
Many nights lost in despair
Countless tears
Cashed in for another's gain
Pointing fingers
Really, who is to blame?
Proclaiming Christianity
Nevertheless, going against Christ's name
For you my brother
Should look upon yourself
Through the mirrors
Reflecting with one's own sins
Proclaimed
Is not this so true
Christ already proclaimed
That our sisters and brothers
Will stand aside
Blaming others for faults
They themselves try to hide
I claim no perfection

Trying to account for my own life
My own mistakes
Each step I take in stride
Taking comfort with Christ's promise
I shall never forget
Something stated so simply
Beyond our own sins
Acceptance
Trial
Amnesty

Starting today, consider at least one other individuals spirit that you come encounter with.

I mean really look into that person's soul. Look into their eyes. Can you sense their true spirit? Go beyond that person's appearance. Remember looks can be unreliable. First impressions are important, but take in to consideration that this person is a living, breathing spirit. He or she has feelings, and needs, just like you. Some individuals are more fortunate than others are. Humor is frequently found at someone else's expense. It is just as bad to judge someone behind their backs, as it is to downgrade them, with actions or words to their face. With my experiences in this subject, the hurtfulness from being judged is tremendous, and even if you talk about another individual negatively behind closed doors assuming your words are not heard by the individual you are speaking of, eventually the hurt works its way back. It may not be received by the original ear of the person you were talking about, but it does create a negative force within yourself, as well as the others engaging in the conversation. The outcome is detrimental, causing a "chain reaction". What most people do not realize is that as soon as you converse, or better yet judge another, you are subconsciously giving your spirit consent, and other spirits consent to mock and judge others. It is a completely different story when the person being judged is you. Begin to condition yourself with the ability to remember the feelings experienced through hurtful moments, which you have encountered, and think before you speak badly of another spirit.

"And as ye would that men should do to you, do ye also to them likewise". (Luke 6:31)

"Thou hypocrite, first cast out the beam out of thine own eye; and then shall thou see clearly to cast out the mote out of thy brother's eye". (Matthew 7:5)

"Judge not, and ye shall not be judged: condemn not, and ye shall not be condemned: forgive, and ye shall be forgiven". (Luke 6:37)

"Therefore thou art inexcusable, O man, whosoever thou art that judgest: for wherein thou judgest another, thou condemnest thyself; for thou that judgest doest the same things." (Romans 2:1)

"Thy righteousness is like the great mountains; thy judgments are a great deep: O Lord, thou preservest man and beast" (Psalm 36:6)

Chapter 4
"Follow Christ's Lead"

Force against oppression
Enlighten the world with humbleness
Go at your own pace
Before long it will come naturally
Changing the course
That has been diverted
With the experiences of the world
And Satan's deceit
It is not a simple task
This is clearly hypocritical to the morals
And understandings, we are born with
Forgetting as we gasp the first breath
Upon delivery
Like a dream sometimes fading rapidly
Trying to recall
The details
However, feeling the emotions
Through out the day
With sudden and limited glimpses

Of the choices, we have made
Yesterday only matters
With the mistakes we change
Doing for others
Without expectation
Of gain

Tyranny continues to be constantly fought for, regardless of ones own opinions, religious morals, and beliefs. It is a battle between different forces and the influences of different spirits. The sad thing is and the cause of the increase of confusion and stress in this world is not only the journey of mankind that occurs naturally, but the increased selfishness and desires that individuals are acting upon more frequently and persistently today. From observations I have made, and from personal experiences, I believe that the increased surge in this already rushed world is being caused not only with Satan's torturing influence and very colorful lure, but is also being caused and allowed by spirits that have usually been broken down by the forces of other spirits. In some cases, these spirits may have been subjected to negative forces of other spirits, for several years.

Alternatively, maybe they have experienced just bits and pieces of the puzzle of deciphering the meaning of life and what really is good versus evil. What is right from wrong? I believe we are all created equally. In addition, this great journey begins beyond the sudden entry in to the verge of mortality.

"For with God nothing shall be impossible" (Luke 1:37)

The spirit holds an incredible amount of knowledge prior to beginning the steps along with other worldly beings. What about feelings? And emotions? What about the feelings that goes along with good verses evil? Feeling the senses that go along with experiencing the forces amongst ourselves, can help us understand and built the defense against the spirit breakers.

Feel sorrow: "Sorrow is better than laughter: for by the sadness of the countenance the heart is made better". (Ecclesiastes 7:3)

Have we experienced the emotion of anger prior to birth? "Cease from anger, and forsake wrath; fret not thyself in any wise to do evil". (Psalms 37:8)

"Be not hasty in thy spirit to be angry: for anger resteth in the bosom of fools". (Ecclesiastes 7:9)

"For the wrath of man worketh not the righteousness of God". (James 1:20)

"What about the belligerence we inflict upon one another?

I wonder if compassion has ever really been felt or expressed, as it should be. Compassion is something that this world could sure use a lot more of. Positive attitude is greatly lacking in society today as well. It is hard to have a positive attitude, if anger and disappointment is continually darkening your path. Anger breaks us down leading to disappointment. Causing a chain reaction. There is a increase on a daily basis to the continual spiral, which I have experienced personally, and have contributed to falling downward, with each of us adding to the links of the endless chain, not considering the selfishness, lack of compassion, not realizing the true worth of other spirits in our lives, as well as our own spirit. Resulting in the destruction of ourselves, as well as others. It is possible to follow a more positive pathway that can be a rewarding accomplishment, our soul's final challenge, and imagine the outcome with positive team effort. I am a firm believer in Aristotle's writings and teachings. In studying Aristotle I enjoy the methods he built in regards of argument to influence and persuasion. With this he explored and perfected what he called the three levels of persuasion.

Aristotle's Three Levels of Persuasion

1) **Logos: (Is in reference to Logical) this was Aristotle's preferred approach to persuasion. This level of persuasion is by the use of reasoning (Logical reasoning).**

2) **Pathos: (Is in reference to Emotions, Feelings, Passion, and Empathy). Pathos is like a two-sided coin, it can be used through positive emotions and negative emotions.**

3) **Ethos: (Is in reference to Ethics) Ethos come from within ourselves, our own built- in moral code.**

You are probably asking yourself at this very moment why I am bringing up Aristotle's levels of persuasion. Especially since the title of this chapters poem is "Follow Christ's Lead". As many of you know Aristotle was born in 384

B.C., but what I find interesting is that as Aristotle not being a religious man, he did believe in God, and identified God as the premier being. Aristotle was a virtuous spirit and believed that in following the ways of God was ones own spirits way of reaching beyond this mortal world in becoming God-like. So obviously Aristotle was born with knowledge of knowing what is right from wrong. His footprints were sketched upon the earth before God's son Christ's destiny to save humanity, and cleanse the sinners and their UN yet born. By studying the scriptures, and many great philosophers throughout time, we can recognize the importance of equality and acceptance. There are vast approaches of enlightening your spirit and building your spirit up. We are all as lamplights of truth to bring light to the darkened, to teach everyone, especially the claimed "unreachable". Let us all join together in the regime of the defense against the spirit breakers. Spirits get sidetracked through the everyday routines of this mortal world. Even as us being equal as spirits, each spirit does have their own unique manner in falling back in line with the spirit builders, this is where Aristotle's Three Levels of Persuasion comes in: ex; some spirits are more logical than others, where as ethics or moral beliefs have an impact on certain spirits, and other spirits respond emotionally, but remember to use positive approaches not negative ones. And I can not state this enough: "Practice dignity instead of deceit". Every spirit is approachable, it is in the manner in which we reach out to one another that makes the positive difference. We can make a difference! We can lead a definite change!

Chapter 5
"Vanity"

Well yes, this is true
It is in me
It is in you
Such bribery
Highway robbery
Starting from the beginning
What matters is the ending
What lies in between?
At moments
Rushes go through me
Almost bursting from the seams
And then suddenly
I am being slapped across the face
With feelings of another
So much like the same
What a spectacle
Worn upon our sleeves
Along with this, could vanity
Have a twin named Greed?
Vanity
Justification for Deceit
Philanthropy pushed aside
This act of violence
Some incidents considered
Lighter
Hasten your speed
Nevertheless, remain humble
Do not join the others side

Individual persona
Is still attractive
Do not take the easy way
Again, remain humble
Encouraging others
Do not hide behind the Devil's guise
Excuses are your first mistake
Everyday giving consent to acts
With hidden meanings
Foresee the prose
From many fine writers before us
With calming compositions
One should not refrain
Nevertheless, we still do
With so many
We complain
Causing the friction
Of the fire
It has started!
Without the acknowledgement of the flame
Beginners bask in the heated array
It is a planned agreement
We have all made
Are you ready?
For the completion of these sins
That we partake
Abandoning
Ones true beliefs
Exceeding further into treachery
Forgetting one another's needs
For ones own selfishness
And deceitful gluttony

"Surely every man walketh in a vain shrew: surely they are disquieted in vain: he heapeth up riches, and knoweth not who shall gather them". (Psalm 39:6) "Remove thy stroke away from me: I am consumed by the blow of thine hand".
(Psalm 39:10)

"When thou with rebukes dost correct man for iniquity, thou makest his beauty to consume away like a moth: surely every man is vanity". (Psalm 39:11)

"The Lord knoweth the thoughts of man, that they are vanity". (Psalm 94:11)

Amongst the panic and ruin, all worldly things disintegrate, even our mortal bodies deteriorate. Starting with selfishness, when does "self love" begin? As soon as ones eyes first open, immediately seeking gain, and direction. This is the beginning of the diversion.

That which is evil we should refrain. Stop following the unsighted, along Satan's guided way. Remain true to Christ's teachings. Excepting ones own mistakes, and learning along the way. Realize others around you, and their needs. Practice dignity instead of deceit. Realizing your true worth will allow you to accept the true spirit of others. Realize the balance of self-love in a moderate, humble way. Appreciate the equal-ness of our neighbors as ourselves.

"Thou shalt love the Lord thy God with all thy heart, and with all thy soul, and with all thy mind". (Matthew 23:37)

"This is the first and great commandment". (Matthew 23:38)

"And the second is like unto it, Thou shalt love thy neighbor as thyself". (Matthew 23:39)

"Beloved, let us love one another: for love is of God; and every one that loveth is born of God, and knoweth God". (1 John 4:7)

Chapter 6
"Within The Haze of Deception"

Clouded footsteps
Unguided way
As much as I hope
The tainted remnants
Of actions
From my past
Still remain
I have tried
But the facts
Never change
My direction
And actions
By my own freewill
Knowing
However
Not heeding
Denying
Not believing
Many excuses
I have made
I have turned
Around
Possibly
Not even half way
My strength
That is weakened
Endurance regained
Even in spite of my worldly ways

I try
To focus
Slowly
I awaken
Amongst the mist
Which
Seems to subside
My prayers
That seem unanswered
Now faintly
Growing stronger
A light
Now as my guide
For this is what Christ
Died for
Amongst all of the selfishness
And mans visible pride
A soul so rebellious
Granted
Direction
Without restraint
By the one
Who gave everything
His Life
Through bloodshed
And hate

So many times, I have found myself going through life with my head in the clouds, sopping up the precipitation of others around me, regardless of the negativity, and the severity of the storm, I have been drenched with the confusion of distasteful opinions and beliefs. Imagine the rainbows that I have missed, while falling into the darkness, instead of enjoying the clarity of the downpour of God's blessings upon me. I intend to dance in the rain, and share my direction with other spirits in my life. As I said before, "Practice dignity instead of deceit".

"My lips shall not speak wickedness, nor my tongue utter deceit". (Job 27:4)

"He that worketh deceit shall not dwell within my house: he that telleth lies shall not tarry in my sight". (Psalms 101:7)

"Beware lest any man spoil you through philosophy and vain deceit, after the tradition of men, after the rudiments of the world, and not after Christ". (Colossians 1:8)

Chapter 7
"Suspicious Serpent"

Unravel evil one
Show yourself
Untangle
Ambiguous slithering
Leader of Confusion
Descend
Now plunge
Slide Down
Hasty
Go Steadfast
Get Thee Hence!
You have broken down
Deceived the weary
Through the decades
Through attacks
Through events
With disbelieving
I have slipped
Not this time
The time is now!
The right time
Go!
Fall!
Diminish!
No more Disorientation!
You and yours
Limited
Rein no more!

Under falsification
Christ abides true
He has risen
I cannot
I will not accept
The lies
This is not the same for you!
Descend!
Once again
Get Thee Hence!
Satan

Satan thrives on deception, and pain. He and his followers are constantly trying to blind us and erase our minds of the knowledge of what is right from wrong. The diversion becomes more so with the steady increase of confusion, with the rapid changing of the times. Day after day, time goes by faster, and our spirits forget about what is important. With this we take so much for granted, and just think of ourselves, and ones own personal gain. Moreover, this is only part of how Satan and his followers succeed. Evil is alluring.

Avoid halfhearted attempts. This does not mean that you cannot start with small steps, but you need to have the desire to seriously begin to defend yourself, your children, family, and friends, and other spirits (that you encounter along the walk through life.) against the spirit breakers. Begin building the strength of your mind. By doing this you will be able to change, the negative thoughts that instantly arise. Changing your thought process with positive, and kind thoughts will have an amazing effect within yourself, and a great influence upon others. Start changing the direction of the chain reaction, from a negative force to a positive one. By setting this positive example an amazing force will be build up against the spirit breakers whom are constantly attempting to destroy the good which all of us have within us. We all possess greatness, and are free to choose to use our spirit to enlighten or darken the pathway for ourselves, and for others.

"Ye serpents, ye generation of vipers, how can ye escape the damnation of hell?"
(St. Matthew 23:33)

"None called for justice, nor any pleaded for truth: they trust in vanity, and speak lies; they conceive mischief, and bring forth iniquity". (Isaiah 59:4)

"He that devises to do evil shall be called a mischievous person". (Proverbs 24:8)

Chapter 8
"Hell"

Satan entices
Followers
With deception
Suave effects
Darkness
Drowns out any light
Recruiting servants
Constantly await
Jumping at any point
Any opportunity
To clench you
Between their hot
Deadened digits
Their figures altering
For every occasion
Satan's followers lean
On the brinks of hell
Falling in to despair
Empty Caracas's
Burning
In anticipation
Of victims
Marketed souls
Fall
Into
Despair
Lifeless bodies
Once

Twice
Amongst
Lies
Deceit
Satan's advertisements
Only he shall reap
The value of a spirit
Cannot be measured
Even yet
Christ remains
Offering his hand
Beyond any degree
The fire scorching him
Beyond recognition
As time
Moves
Quicker
We
Fail to see
The Savior
Of our souls
Many questions
Answered
Unheard
Useless
Not only
Are we blinded
Acoustic rhythm
Has been stolen
As spirits,
Still
Selling souls

This frightens me. Which can be a positive emotion, if you use it to stay clear from Satan's experienced whispers. Many times I myself fail to see Christ's light. That is why we all have the sixth sense. Now, with the hurried bustle of this world, as you are changing your thoughts, which in turn will change your reactions with others, start looking others in their eyes, when you encounter them. Stop and consider these other spirits, of not only yourself, your own wants, and desires. Actually consider the feelings of these other spirits in spite of your own. It has been said many times, that the eyes of an individual are the windows to ones soul. This is true. So much can be learned through the eyes of another. Have you ever noticed the positive gleam of another individual's eyes, when their spirit is filled with joy and excitement? On the other hand, how about another individuals eyes when their spirit is filled with sorrow or disappointment? Even with accompanied tears, every spirits eyes, changes with different moods, and experiences.

There is definitely a difference in the spirits eyes, with the changing of emotions. The tears of happiness of ones eyes, differ from that of the tears of sorrow, or pain. Take notice of other spirits that you encounter, their eyes speak without words. Usually when an individual does not look you in the eyes, trust should be questioned. Even the eyes of a shy spirit, differ from the eyes, of a spirit practicing lies and deceit. Take heed of the eyes of shame and guilt, for within these spirits, a conscience still remains. A spirit with a conscience can still be saved. Break the chains of Satan's reactions, and control. Christ's truth remains. Each one of us is instilled with the knowledge of the difference between right and wrong, and what is good verses evil. The sad thing is we all continue to make excuses, turning our backs against our redeemer, our fellow spirits, and consequently we allow Satan, and his followers, to distort, and cloud our vision, against the right chosen path through this mortal life. Unbelievably these days are limited, but there is still time, to defend yourself against the spirit breakers. If you and each spirit you come in contact with have a positive, and caring spirit, and react in a more positive manner, to experiences, and taking other's feelings and needs in to consideration, the force of defense will grow stronger against Satan and his followers, against the spirit breakers. We can defend each other, lowering and preventing the number of Satan's followers. See we all have the freedom of choosing to be a positive spirit, or a spirit breaker. Every spirit has the capability of darkening their spirit, and other spirits that they encounter. Moreover, each spirit has the choice of following Christ's lead, the guided way. Enlightening the path for other spirits to God's celestial gates.

"The light of the body is the eye: if therefore thine eye be single, thy whole body shall be full of light" (St. Matthew 6:22)

"But if thine eye be evil, thy whole body shall be full of darkness. If therefore the light that is in thee be darkness, how great is that darkness!" (St. Matthew 6:23)

"But the fearful, and unbelieving, and the abominable, and murderers, and whoremongers, and sorcerers, and idolaters, and all liars, shall have their part in the lake which burns with fire and brimstone: which is the second death" (Revelation 21:8)

"And cast ye the unprofitable servant into outer darkness: there shall be weeping and gnashing of teeth" (St. Matthew 25:30)

"And fear not them which kill the body, but are not able to kill the soul: but rather fear him which is able to destroy both soul and body in hell" (St. Matthew 10:28)

I cannot emphasis enough to practice dignity instead of deceit, to love one another, and follow Christ's lead.

"Let the words of my mouth, and the meditation of my heart, be acceptable in thy sight, O Lord, my strength, and my redeemer" (Psalms 19:14)

"Blessed are they which are persecuted for righteousness' sake: for theirs is the kingdom of heaven" (St. Matthew 5:10)

"And be not conformed to this world: but be ye transformed by the renewing of your mind, that ye may prove what is that good, and acceptable, and perfect, will of God" (Romans 12:2)

Chapter 9
"Anguish in the Rush"

Against life's
Once heightened augur
Falling downward
With others slander
Haste
Without thinking
Words breaking silence
Without speaking
Practice what you preach
Instead of the many masks
Each person wears
Most likely
Containing more than deceit
Look into my eyes
If only for a moment
Grommet
The weaves of worldly ways
Host
After disgruntled promise
Only moans
Of perpetual whiners
Can be heard
Amongst the scurry
My fellow brothers and sisters
Forever anguish in the rush
Losing ones true self
Into the worldly hurry

Notice the apparent! Ok, when I say notice, I do not just mean glance at things and happenings around you. Take heed. Do you know what taking heed means? Pay attention!

Do not ignore the obvious! The time has come to even take note of what seems like little things. The sad thing is that what you and I take as little things, and unimportant, are the opening spaces, where the spirit breakers are intentionally slipping in. They want us not to notice. While we are, yes, you and I are trying to keep up with all the craziness of this world, believing that we are "keeping up". Trying to do the best we can. The spirit breakers are taking every opportunity to get the upper hand, and in addition break us down. And sad to say, that with the deceit of the spirit breakers, individuals that are believing that they are "surviving", are pushed into becoming spirit breakers. This is what Satan wants also. We are blinded. And the spirit breakers are coming in from all sides. We are living in a time which is ticking away faster and faster.

Believing that we are keeping up in regards to society, career, and religion. If you ask how, it can be through politics and government, religion, and let us not forget health issues, and insurance companies', etcetera. In regards to these groups, and their influences that affect more less everyone, the impact is not only morally wrong, but has many people blindsided on limited information. Tie up all loose ends. Moreover, do not just take this lightly! Double, Triple, and if you have to keep checking, and protecting yourself, and others. Do so! Building the defense against the spirit breakers. We can defend each other by lowering and preventing the number of Satan's followers, and their fraudulent gains. See we all have the freedom of choosing to be a spirit builder, or a spirit breaker. It is really quite simple, it takes work and a lot of practice. Before you know it the dignified defense will come naturally.

"For such are false apostles, deceitful workers, transforming themselves into the apostles of Christ" (II Corinthians 12:13)

"Beware of false prophets, which come to you in sheep's clothing, but inwardly they are ravening wolves" (St. Matthew 7:15)

"Neither give place to the devil" (Ephesians 4:27)

"Let him that stole steal no more: but rather let him labor, working good, that he may have to give to him that needeth" (Ephesians 4:28)

"And have no fellowship with unfruitful works of darkness, but rather reprove them" (Ephesians 5:11)

Chapter 10
"The Root of All Evil"

Derivation
Surrounded by power
Unholy Restrictions
Increasing
Velocity
Of corruption
Altered borders
Through dishonesty
Resulting
In distortion
Causing friction
Turning of the wheels
Against
And
With the rapid
Timeframe
We are all under duress
Yet
Thinking we are
"Keeping up".
Abide by
Christ's teachings
Take Vigilance!
This is Satan's bribery
Making promises
Unfulfilled
Materialistic
Acquisitive

Trophies
Seizing
This means taking!
From
"The less fortunate"
For evil's self gain
Yet
Self-love
Arrogance
Is much poorer
Then the spirits
In which are looked upon
With pointed fingers
And blame
Estranged
Mortal Amusement
Through someone else's
Heartache
Currency
Taken;
Exchanged
By the hands
Of those who claim
To save
These so-called leaders
Declaring fictitious rank!
Weep not!
Christ's brothers and sisters
For you shall see the day
And the limits
Of your mortal body's
Will be rewarded

With astonishing multitude
Of
Infinite sacred gain
Believe in God's direction
Do not give up
Do not turn away
Remain Steadfast
Persevere
Avoiding Satan's lure
Evade
Avoid all roots of evil

"For the love of money is the root of all evil: which
while some coveted after, they have erred from the faith,
and pierced themselves through with many sorrows."
(II Timothy 6:10)

"Perverse disputing of men of corrupt minds, and
destitute of the truth, supposing that gain is godliness,
from such withdraw thyself."
(II Timothy 6:5)

"But thou, O man of God, flee these things; and follow
after righteousness, godliness, faith, love, patience,
meekness."
(II Timothy 6:11)

Chapter 11
"Wisdom"

Empty Casks are building up against me
Inside me
Like a fine vintage wine
Moments
Seconds
Minutes
My life has become so refined
Through this
And from my past
Images
Echoes
Shattered against the metaphors in my mind
My feet infrequently on the ground
With unpaved
Unguided paths
I have been torn
I have been tainted
Is it possible to be reborn?
Or is that the proper term?
If truth be told
We all have the paraphernalia instilled inside us
Within us
From the beginning
Through the end
It is a matter of realization
A process which is flowing
Endlessly
Progressively
Until the end

We acquire wisdom every second, of every moment, of every hour, of every day, and through the cascades of our subconscious, our dreams, yet wisdom has been instilled within us since the beginning of time.

A mind of a true scholar is not formed or found roaming behind the walls of a concrete building, or learned amongst the pages of other's philosophies, but within oneself in the manner of how we treat one another, and finding one's final posture… Open your mind-

Gain knowledge of other's before us, and press on, beyond our brother's and sister's threshold, giving to other's, forming true: "Life". This is for Gandhi.

"A hypocrite with his mouth destroyeth his neighbor: but through knowledge shall the just be delivered" (Proverbs 12:9)

"He that is void of wisdom despiseth his neighbor: but the man of understanding holdeth his peace" (Proverbs 12:12)

"The fruit of the righteous is a tree of life; and he that winneth souls is wise" (Proverbs 12:30)

"He that walketh with wise men shall be wise: but a companion of fools shall be destroyed" (Proverbs 13:20)

"The fear of the Lord is the instruction of wisdom; and before honor is humility" (Proverbs 15:33)

"An ungodly man diggeth up evil: and in his lips there is a burning fire" (Proverbs 16:27)

Chapter 12
"Somewhere"

My mind wanders
Muse
What is this all about?
The distance seems to grow
More distant
You are quite
Far away
Allay…
Drift
It hurts
Do you pray?
Do you believe?
That prayers
Are answered?
Beyond
All the confusion
A slow
Yet subtle
Train
Falling off track
From the obvious
Faith still remains.

If you had a ticket to go anywhere where would you go? Imagine your life as your spirit being on a perpetual train. Can you hear the engine roar? It's fleet entangled inside are all God's spirits. It's voyage is your life, as the iron wheels turn and the velocity becomes faster, the sparks flying as they slide against the tracks through night and hours of daylight ticking away, with only flashes through the images in your mind, looking through your eyes, which are the windows of your soul, you catch only glimpses of the entire picture, with only transparency of your life situations as the train slows down, turning upon every curve, and stopping at different posts in your life. Sometimes the train smoothly comes to a halt, and at other points comes to an abrupt stop. Through the perplexity of your life's destinations you are also crowded and pushed aside as other spirit's force themselves in front of you to obtain their position both off the train as well as on. Now imagine purchasing another ticket, the previous train plunges off upon the tracks. You decide to change trains, and embark upon a different set of tracks. It is amazing the difference you feel, a sense of relief as you gather your senses and board the new train. As the ticket man tears the ticket apart and hands you your half the scenery begins to change, your mind becomes clearer, and the world around you has a brighter look and calmness to it. Other spirit's around you smile and welcome you aboard. An announcement is made overhead of the news of the train you were previously traveling upon had just derailed. Time is still on your side! Whoa! Finding myself in this situation I would say a prayer to thank God for sparing my life and to please give strength to the lost spirit's who you were traveling with just momentarily, to somehow still find a way into God's light.

This reminds me of a quote made by Aristophanes: "Your lost friends are not dead, but gone before, advanced a stage or two upon that road which you must travel in the steps they trod."

"Train up a child in the way he should go: and when he is old, he will not depart from it". (Proverbs 22:6)

Chapter 13
"Force Built With Pain"

I no longer stare at the walls
Time spend
Countless hours
I am surprised
Some should have fallen
I have sown my seeds
Desisted
Desirability
Sour taste
Still left
In my mouth
Semi-sweet
Comfort
From another's deceit?
No further apologies
Forgiven
Time is running out.
I cannot spend my time worrying
About those who love me
Against those who hate me
You do not even know me
What matters most is
I like myself
Finally!
I have found what
Matters
I've discovered my
Inner Peace.

Pain comes in countless forms. Pain can be received or delivered amongst spirits, but personally, I believe the worst pain is the self-destruction that we create within ourselves, or to ourselves, which most likely causes us to want to inflict pain upon other spirits, because of the misery, either knowingly or not. It reminds me of the saying that misery likes company. Satan thrives on misery. If we are not happy with our spirits, why would we want to be alone? Moreover, diffuse into disgrace? Then we find other means of numbing ourselves from our own pain and dissolution, through alcohol, drugs, sex, and other indulgences in regards to money through worldly gain. It is time to let go of our worldly restraints, and regain our true spirits, the reality of this mortal world is sometimes too much to bear, but through dazed minds, and blurred eyes Satan is bound to break our spirits down. Find the peace within your spirit and share the peace you have obtained with other spirits you encounter. "Be a spirit builder not a spirit breaker".

"For I reckon that the sufferings of this present time are
not worthy to be compared with the glory which shall
be revealed in us."
(Romans 8:18)

"And the fruit of righteousness is sown in peace of them
that make peace."
(James 3:18)

"If we confess our sins, he is faithful and just to forgive us our sins, and to cleanse us from all the unrighteousness."
(John 1:9)

"Peace be to the brethren, and love with faith, from God the Father and the Lord Jesus Christ."
(Ephesians 6:23)

Chapter 14
"Restraining Timepiece"

Within this space of earth and mind
Ones search for worth is hard to find
Somebody else's desire
May not be the same
One Mans disappointment might be another ones gain
Only the strong will still endeavor
Evils own demise
By one so clever
A spirit that surrounds everything
Forever
An ambiance so divine
With arms and hands reached limitlessly
Are they invisible?
Do we decline to see?
Perhaps too weak to protest or believe
Later falling into pride and deceit
This is true of ones own self love
Even stronger then the love
For our Guardian above
Leading to ones last day
The finale
Moments set forever in Ruin
Satan believes
That evil will succeed
From Christ's own blood
We shall prevail
This is now
This is Hell

Amongst the ruin
I can still see
The sun
Running from fear
Within Hells confusion
Forewarning ignored
Living in a illusion
This is only the beginning
Of what is yet to come
Omen
Look around
Take notice of the signs
These are the days
The last of the times

Aristotle: "The entire heaven is one and eternal (aidios)
having neither beginning nor end of an entire aion'".

Chapter 15
"Gait to Die"

To bare forgiveness to the skies
Torture like no other can claim
For what seems so much to the blessed as the same
Do you understand the difference?
Be au fait with the gift
His blood taken
For Mans uplift
Impure spirits given
More than a second chance
Backstabbing cartel
Twofaced parasites unhesitatingly spit
For what?
His life given
For all others sins
His linger
To proclaim
Gods love
Through his light
Upon this defiant
Darkened world
Gilded upon his face
Light radiates
Self-sacrificed love
Forever shines
From Calvary

Can you imagine the pain that Christ was feeling at
the time of his death? Not only physically, but the

humiliation, the heartache of being slain by individuals that he had spend time with and had befriended while harmoniously praising the words of God? Jesus chose to become human; he worked amongst the poverty stricken, sick, and the cast outs of society. Jesus volunteered to sacrifice his already angelic honor, stepping down from the kingdom of God. Jesus Christ embarked upon the journey of journeys as he relinquished his position of Gods right hand, to come to earth, (a world so marred with darkness and hate) to lead the mortal world back to redemption. Christ's spirit was abundant with faith then, and his conviction in our spirits continues even after his ascendance from the cross 2,000 years ago.

"Deliver me out of the mire, and let me not sink: let me be delivered from them that hate me, and out of the deep waters." (Psalms 69-14)

Chapter 16
"Satirize"

Why the mocking?
I wish
I could express
The sadness
I contain
I hold
What have I done
To be treated in this way
And I confess
No perfection
I know now
It is okay
In your opinion
I have strayed
Beyond what realms
Have you heard of perjury
The lines are being crossed
Tainted
No longer take the time
No more tears
Wasted
For another's amusement
Laugh
Laugh
I am breaking away
Gratis
Nothing owed
Goodbye is too valuable

"Thy faith hath saved thee; go in peace". (St. Luke 7:50)

"Those by the wayside are they that hear; then cometh the devil, and taketh away the word of their hearts, lest they should believe and be saved". (St. Luke 8:12)

Chapter 17
"Disillusionment"

One question for you
What have you learned
Through all of this confusion
I
Slip from regret
Why
Can not all
respect
Blaming
Disorder
On the hearts of others
I can not recognize you
As my brother
Trip
Into the plunder
I await
The day
To say
I am sorry
For you
Can you
Believe
In me
There is more then one
Not just your way of thinking
We all have
Restraints
We are all beautiful
We are all God's children

If I could reach out to everyone that I have offended throughout my life I would. I have had the opportunity to apologize to many individuals. It is my greatest hope that they can accept my act of apology with true conviction, and that they are able to forgive me full heartedly. It is amazing what an immense release it is within my heart and an uplift of my spirit from the weight that I have carried upon my shoulders for years. To be able to be forgiven is one of the greatest gifts that I have received. Growing up in society today seems to be getting worse than ever, even though when I was a child there were a lot of hurtful experiences that I encountered, as well as participated in. I realize that as children we do not really take into consideration the impact that we can have upon one another. Words and actions can have a great impact upon an individuals life forever, sometimes impacting that spirits potential to be limited, and not obtain the success that all spirits deserve in life. There is a fine perimeter between being confident and being successful throughout life, as well as feeling limited through the breaking down of ones spirit through other spirits. I can not emphasize enough the importance of building up other spirits. Parents teach your children reverent conduct, explain to your children the importance of every spirit. Every spirit has a place in this world. As adults we are responsible to lead our children, as well as every other spirit's that we come in contact with to enlighten and build their spirits up. Remember the chain reaction? My fellow spirits practice dignity instead of deceit.

"Humble yourselves in the sight of the Lord, and he shall lift you up". (St. James 4:10)

"My little children, let us not love in word, neither in tongue; but in deed and in truth".
(I St. John 3:18)

"Beloved, follow not that which is evil, but that which is good. He that doeth good is of God: but he that doeth evil hath not seen God". (The Third Epistle of John verse 11)

Chapter 18
"Release the Demons"

Everyone has fallen in some way
I myself fall everyday
Sometimes in ways
That only I can see
The problem is
We stop to believe
Wait
Turn
The other way around
It is a two edged sword
Not believing in ones self
Converging in the midst of
Pessimistic hordes
Causing our destruction
Since we were born
Egoism
Neglecting humanity
Submit accordingly
Pray
Always pray
As often as you can.

I am a firm believer in prayer, I have had many moments when I have wanted to just collapse and just let go of everything around me. I believe that all spirits have that feeling at some point if not innumerable times in their life within this mortal world. I find solace in prayer. When praying you should really focus and try to tune out the environment around you. If it is possible find a peaceful and private place and get on your knees, this is the proper most respectful manner in which to request Gods direction, but this is not the only way to pray, you can pray anywhere, anytime of day or night. When praying do not just focus on your needs and desires. Thank God for your spirits existence and the blessings in which he has bestowed upon you and your loved ones, as well as the rest of the world, pray for direction and comfort for all spirits, pray for peace. Do not give up regardless of how depleted of circumstances that you may find yourself in. Remember to light the path for other spirits, give of yourself unselfishly.

"Never, never, never give up". (Winston Churchill 1941)

"Is any among you afflicted? Let him pray. Is any merry? Let him sing psalms".
(James 5:13)

"But thou, when thou prayest, enter into thy closet, and when thou hast shut the door, pray to thy father which is in secret; and thy Father which seeth in secret shall reward thee openly". (St. Matthew 6:6)

Chapter 19
"Apostasy Overruled"

Upon the harbor
Of needed evoke
With words being spoken
Without care of original meaning
With thy neighbors
Being judged
Against one another
We practice
Deceiving
No care of hurting
Another
No longer believing
Step back
Turn around
Take heed in the warnings
Just because of the different stances
Does not mean different meanings
Let us all stop accusing
Lets learn to accept
To take responsibility
For the steps each individual takes
No longer forsaking
What is right
Gyrate
See face to face
Christ's teachings
Never change
Even with the sudden lapses

Of time
Remember
These words
Seek and ye shall find
Just open your eyes
Building the force
Against evil
There is still time
We shall win!
And meet
Once again
Family
Friends
Who have already entered
The gates
Of Gods mansion
Forever basking
In the sunny firmament
Within his heavens

The light of messiah will return, with this so many events have and are taking place, distracting all spirits within this mortal spectrum. Through the darkness of the adversary his spirit shines through to all of us. Peace will be acquired again. Gods work is all around us, even with the distraction of hate and selfishness, the final day is coming, to bless every spirit upon this earth. So many great composers and philosophers have spoken of this day, through their music, and writings. The hands of time have spun without delay to bring us to this day of rejoicing. Bring forth your spirit in an uplifting manner, and join hands with the nations of your sisters and brothers spirits. Let go of hate. Give of yourself altruistically. Forgiving the disappointments brought upon yourself as well as by others. Love as you should love. It is within everyone of us. Let your spirit shine. Unity begins with U and I. Tribulation will dissolve, and God's followers will rise above this mortal world and join him. Saints and Sages will combine when the rapture and the second coming preside.

"Thou shalt arise, and have mercy upon Zion: for the time to favor her, yea, for the set time, is come". (Psalms 102:13)

Chapter 20
"Cast Thou Love upon Me Thy Lord"

I still walk
Unsteadily
Still remain
Within these
Mortal walls
Have I served
Ye
All of
My self's
Petulance sentence
Yet
Do I deserve
Thy patience
From several
Times
Past
Repeated
Loathing
I beg
Ye
Save
My soul
I pray
Most humbly
Cast thou
Love
Upon me
Thy Lord

"The grace of our Lord Jesus Christ be with you all.
Amen" (Revelation 22:21)